Technology Partner:

LEDGER

Endorsements

It is time to teach our children wisely about crypto and the future of digital networks of money and value. As a dad, I highly recommend this book!

—Hon. J. Christopher Giancarlo, "CryptoDad," former Chairman of the U.S. Commodity Futures Trading Commission

This book is a guide and an inspiring treasure for tomorrow's visionaries eager to make a positive impact on the world.

—Vincent Chok, Founder and CEO, First Digital

The transformative power of cryptocurrencies is something everyone needs to understand, and kids first! This book is a must-read!

—Pascal Gauthier, CEO, Ledger

A perfect introduction to the world of blockchain and the future of money for the next generation.

—Yat Siu, Chairman and Co-Founder, Animoca Brands

A fun and insightful book that introduces the world of Web3 and cryptocurrency to future generations . . . a must-read.

—Ben Zhou, CEO, Bybit

A must-have for young minds curious about the future of finance and technology.

—Luuk Strijers, CEO, Deribit

This is more than a book, it is a guide and a treasure trove for parents and educators, blending humor and insight as it teaches tomorrow's digital leaders. It's the financial literacy children deserve, delivered in a way they'll love.

—Frederik Gregaard, CEO, Cardano Foundation

A must-read for kids to strive in modern finance.

—Charles d'Haussy, CEO, dYdX Foundation

Decoding Crypto's knack for making complex concepts easy and fun for kids is nothing short of magical. This book turns crypto learning into an adventure!

—Jean-Marie Mognetti, CEO, CoinShares

Fun, educational, and critically important—this book exposes kids to concepts they must understand in our rapidly changing world.

—Farzam Ehsani, Co-Founder and CEO, VALR

Endorsements

A fun and insightful book that enables future generations to learn about the exciting world of crypto.

—Michael Shaulov, CEO, Fireblocks

A fantastic resource for any parent and educator looking to teach kids about money and cryptocurrencies.

—Stefan Kimmel, CEO, M2

This book will enable the future generation to learn about the future of money.

—Sam Tabar, CEO, Bit Digital

As a parent and a founder in the digital assets space, this book is a great introduction for young minds to learn about future money and the systems they will be growing up with.

—Darius Sit, Founder and CIO, QCP

Crypto will be the future of global commerce, but it's incredibly challenging to teach. *Decoding Crypto* masterfully simplifies this.

—Robert Materazzi, CEO, Lukka

Decoding Crypto is foundational for kids growing up in the digital age.

—Jehan Chu, Co-Founder, Kenetic

Decoding Crypto is a must for any parent looking to educate their kids about the exciting world of crypto.

—Talal Tabbaa, CEO, CoinMENA

A must-have for any parent or educator that wants the younger generation to learn about the evolving blockchain and cryptocurrency space correctly, and not from social media mislearnings.

—Joey Garcia, Director, Xapo Bank

If you believe that blockchain and cryptocurrencies are here to stay, you will want your children to be introduced to the topic as early as possible. And this book does that in a fun and engaging way!

—Jean Chalopin, Writer-Producer of TV series including *Inspector Gadget*, *The Mysterious Cities of Gold*, *Ulysses 31*, and *The Real Ghostbusters*

Decoding Crypto with Henri & Hodler

Explaining difficult concepts in a fun and simple way.

WRITTEN BY
Henri Arslanian
Michael Dotsikas

ILLUSTRATED BY
Billy Martin

Decoding Crypto

Brown Books Kids
16250 Knoll Trail Drive, Suite 205
Dallas, Texas 75248
www.BrownBooksKids.com
(972) 381-0009

A New Era in Publishing®

Publisher's Cataloging-In-Publication Data

Names: Arslanian, Henri, author. | Dotsikas, Michael, author. | Martin, Billy (Illustrator), illustrator.
Title: Decoding crypto / written by Henri Arslanian, Michael Dotsikas ; illustrated by Billy Martin.
Description: Dallas, TX ; New York, NY : Brown Books Publishing Group, [2024] | Series: Decoding crypto with Henri & Hodler | Audience: Juvenile. | Summary: Learn about Bitcoin and crypto--whilst having fun! Join crypto-enthusiasts Henri and Hodler as they take an adventurous and fun journey learning about the history and evolution of money and discovering key topics about the future of money, from "Bitcoin" and "Ethereum" to "DeFi" and "NFTs."--Publisher.
Identifiers: ISBN: 978-1-61254-715-2 (hardcover) | 978-1-61254-717-6 (ebook) | LCCN: 2024942438
Subjects: LCSH: Cryptocurrencies--Juvenile literature. | Money--Juvenile literature. | Bitcoin--Juvenile literature. | Blockchains (Databases)--Juvenile literature. | CYAC: Money. | BISAC: JUVENILE NONFICTION / Concepts / Money. | JUVENILE NONFICTION / Business & Economics. | JUVENILE NONFICTION / History / General.
Classification: LCC: HG1710.3 .A77 2024 | DDC: 332.4/048--dc23

This book has been officially leveled by using the
F&P Text Level Gradient™ Leveling System.

ISBN 978-1-61254-715-2
EISBN 978-1-61254-717-6
LCCN 2024942438

Printed in Canada
10 9 8 7 6 5 4 3 2 1

For more information or to contact the authors, please go to https://HenriAndHodler.com.

Dedications & Recognitions

Henri—To my daughter (aka "best friend") and my son (aka "best buddy") for inspiring me to write this book. And to my wife (aka "copilot") for her patience during another crazy project.

Michael—To my wife, Dina, who's my endless inspiration. And to my children: Dream It . . . Believe It . . . Achieve It!

Henri & Michael—And to Satoshi Nakamoto, without whom this book would not be possible.

Special thank you to our contributors:

Anthony Dotsikas (lettering & graphics)
Nelli Mkrtchyan (graphics)
Jenell McLaughlin (contributing editor)

Meet Professor Henri . . .

your classic crypto geek
and delightful nerdy bloke.

And, meet Hodler...

your fine friendly fella
and dashing digital dude.

He's social!

He's hip!

And best of all, he's always in one cool crypto-tutoring **mood!**

Hello there!
If it's crypto knowledge you seek and so desperately yearn . . .
Then you've come to the right place to have fun while you learn.
We're your guides on this journey. It'll be truly worthwhile.
You'll learn all about crypto from two dudes who've got *style!*

We'll explain terms the likes you may not have heard before,
from "Immutable" to "Metaverse" to "Blockchain" and more!
From "Altcoin" to "DeFi" to "Ledger," we've *so-o-o-o-o* much in store!
We'll teach everything crypto . . . with bonus fun facts galore!

Origins of Commerce
But...
before we dive into the makings of this new cryptosphere,
we must examine our past to see how we ended up here.
Let's go back in time to witness where and when commerce was started
to understand how our financial course was historically charted.
As civilizations grew and spread far and wide,
the need for trade and exchange emerged alongside.
Note to Reader: For the words and phrases highlighted in yellow, a detailed definition is provided in the Glossary at the end of the book

First System of Exchange: Barter

Barter, like trading one goat for ten bushels of grain.

Or freshly caught fish for some sweet sugar cane.

Or silky-smooth robes for a dazzling gold chain.

Next Medium of Exchange: Money 

Evolution of Money

Cryptocurrencies
Which brings us to the present, and to this new digital age,
where cryptocurrencies like Bitcoin are now all the rage.
Cryptocurrencies are real money, only in digital form.
They're revolutionizing finance, and they're disrupting the norm.
And just like Hodler, they've taken our planet by digital storm!
Since cryptocurrencies have no physical form, you can't see them or touch them, nor drop them in your piggy bank.
You store them in digital wallets, and can use them to buy toys or candy . . .
or a delicious ballpark frank!
"SMARTPHONES ARE DIGITAL WALLETS"
#1 FAN
Fun Fact!
Digital Wallet
A digital wallet is an app on a smartphone or computer that allows you to hold cryptocurrencies and to pay or transfer without using physical money or cards.

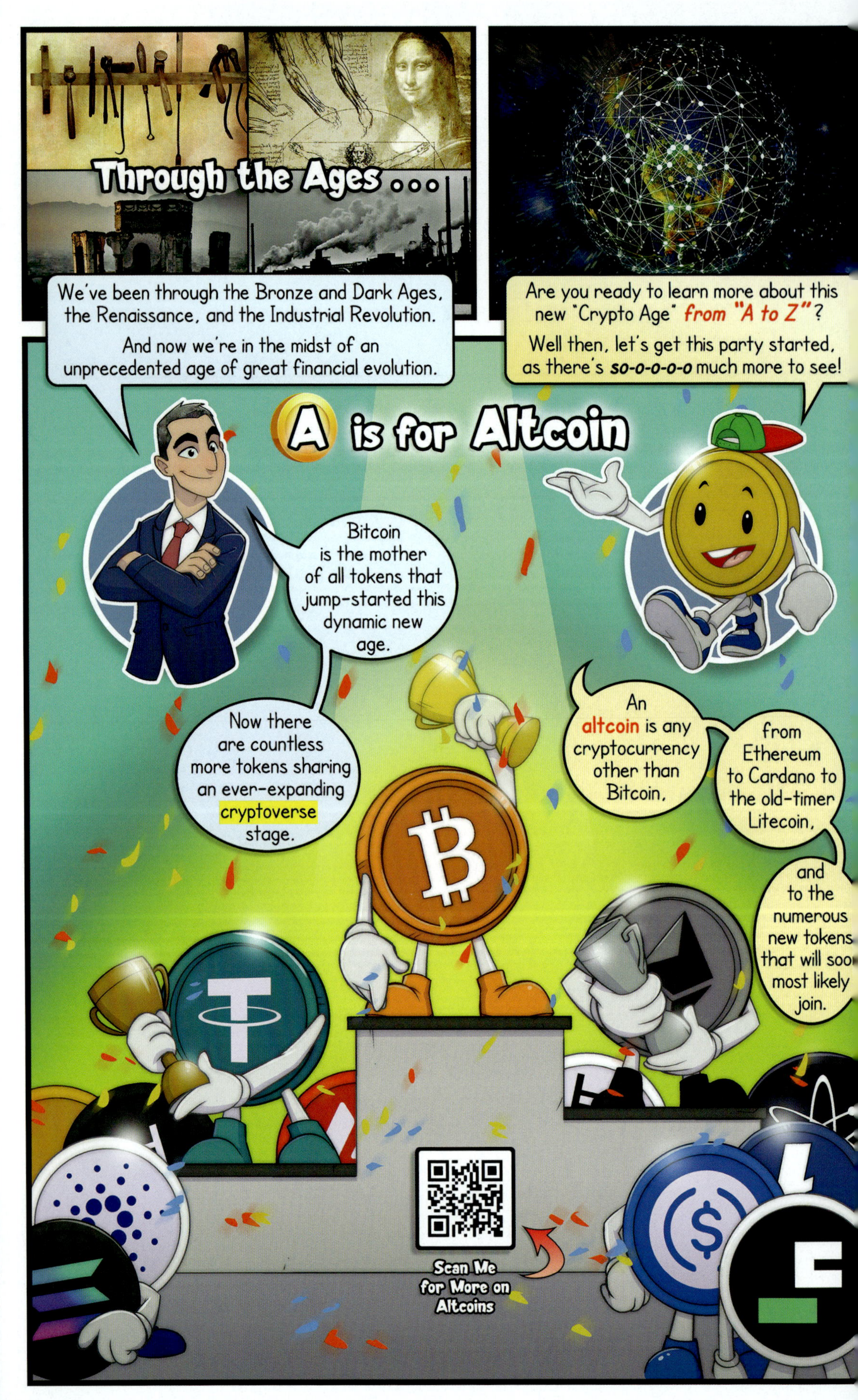
Through the Ages . . .
We've been through the Bronze and Dark Ages, the Renaissance, and the Industrial Revolution.
And now we're in the midst of an unprecedented age of great financial evolution.
Are you ready to learn more about this new "Crypto Age" from "A to Z"?
Well then, let's get this party started, as there's so-o-o-o-o much more to see!
A is for Altcoin
Bitcoin is the mother of all tokens that jump-started this dynamic new age.
Now there are countless more tokens sharing an ever-expanding cryptoverse stage.
An altcoin is any cryptocurrency other than Bitcoin,
from Ethereum to Cardano to the old-timer Litecoin,
and to the numerous new tokens that will soo[n] most likely join.
Scan Me for More on Altcoins

And, let's not forget Dogecoin, our furry, four-legged pal.
She's a popular "meme coin" and one chic superstar gal.
Fun Fact!
Meme Coin
A meme coin is a cryptocurrency often inspired by memes or internet jokes.
While some of these altcoins are strong and robust,
quite many are risky, and some will go
BUST!
List altcoins that you know.

B is for Bitcoin

One Halloween day, in the year 2008, marks a truly historic and significant date.

During a frightening financial crisis amidst grave global despair, the brave and brilliant **Satoshi** emerged with something quite shocking to share.

Satoshi Nakamoto, anonymous Bitcoin creator

Their groundbreaking white paper was cleverly crafted and presented online.

"Bitcoin: A Peer-to-Peer Electronic Cash System" boldly read the headline.

Scan Me for Bitcoin White Paper

Bitcoin is a decentralized digital currency—and the first of its kind. It's not controlled by any government or bank—it's autonomously designed.

It's part of a new monetary system that's simple and clean, and without intermediaries, it's quite efficient and lean.

And ... B is for Blockchain
A blockchain is a secure form of advanced recordkeeping.
It's innovative . . . it's game-changing . . . it's utterly sweeping!
It's a decentralized public financial ledger quite unlike any other,
where every new, successive transaction permanently connects with another.
Every new record combines data from the previous transaction,
which creates unchangeable records, and true, lasting interaction!
All blockchain transactions are sequentially stored in large "data blocks."
And "C-H-A-I-N-E-D" together, like boxcars stocked with locks, clocks, and silly striped socks.
Fun Fact!
Block
Scan Me

C is for

_ _ _ _ _ _ _ _ _ _ _ _ _ _

Use the table below to decode.

Σ &! %©ö

Σö#≠Ω©$ö?≠Ä#

Decoder Table

A – ?	N – ¶
B – €	O – ©
C – Σ	P – ≠
D – ‡	Q – Ø
E – ⁄⁄	R – ö
F – %	S – !
G – $	T – Ω
H – Ä	U – /
I – &	V – ð
J –]	W – ¤
K – ¥	X – 3
L – £	Y – #
M – §	Z – π

The word "cryptocurrency" derives from two distinct words, as a matter of fact.

It's a combination of "cryptography" and "currency," to be more exact.

Scan Me for More on Cryptography

Fun Fact!

Cryptography

Cryptography is the study and practice of techniques for secure communications, and is derived from two Ancient Greek words: "kryptos," which means "hidden" "graphein," which means "to write"

D is for DeFi

DeFi is very different from standard banking and stands for "Decentralized Finance."

It's affecting economies from Armenia to Greece . . .

to croissant-crazy France!

DeFi allows anyone in the world to easily "bank, borrow, and lend."

A smartphone with secure access is about all you'll ever need in the end.

$27.00
0.07171998 ETH
To
0411AD
m&d07282012
SEND NOW

Wow!

Money transactions without the use of a financial institution.

DeFi is DeFinitely DeFining this financial revolution!

Scan Me for More on DeFi

Fun Fact!

Decentralization

Decentralization is a defining characteristic of blockchain technology and refers to the transfer of control and decision-making from a centralized entity, such as a government or bank, to a distributed network of users.

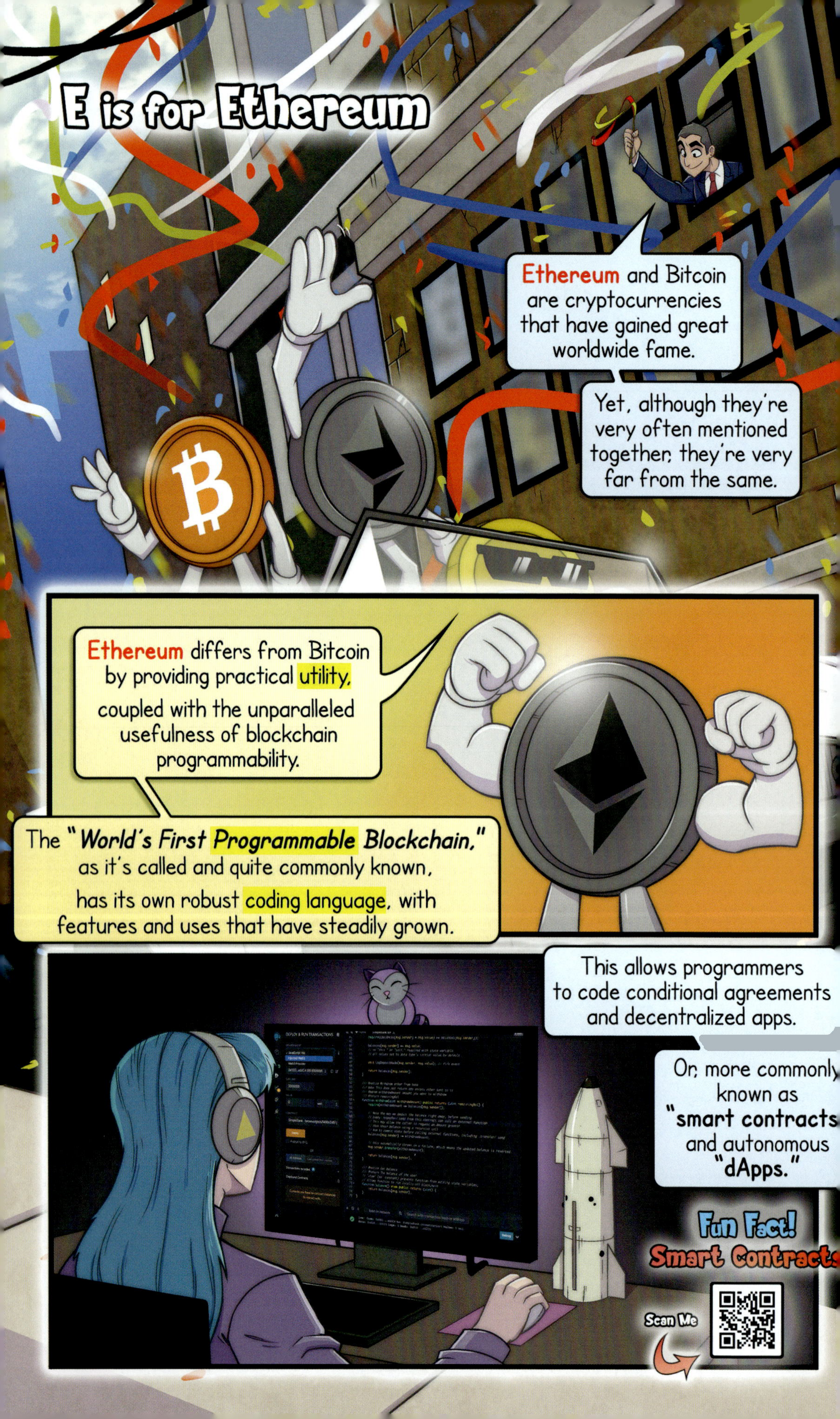

E is for Ethereum

Ethereum and Bitcoin are cryptocurrencies that have gained great worldwide fame.

Yet, although they're very often mentioned together, they're very far from the same.

Ethereum differs from Bitcoin by providing practical utility, coupled with the unparalleled usefulness of blockchain programmability.

The "*World's First Programmable Blockchain,*" as it's called and quite commonly known, has its own robust coding language, with features and uses that have steadily grown.

F is for Fork
Hmm . . . fork?
Aha, got it!
I fancy eating spaghetti and meatballs with my favorite fork.
Good grief ol' chap . . . at times, I truly think you're just one innocent dork.
Henri, please stick to the script, as we're talking "crypto," my friend. Let's explain what "fork" means in crypto. That's what I recommend.
A blockchain fork divides the blockchain and offers you two distinct options to choose.
ETHEREUM
ETHEREUM CLASSIC
Aah . . . just like a fork in the road offers a traveler two distinct pathways to cruise.
A blockchain's stakeholders propose a change to its rules, which splits the blockchain in two,
which then provides another option for which blockchain to use . . . the old or the new.
Hmm . . . it's like tennis, padel, and pickleball, which play fairly the same.
With minor changes to rules and equipment, they're each a distinct game.
What's your favorite sport?
☐ Tennis ☐ Padel ☐ Pickleball

G is for Gas

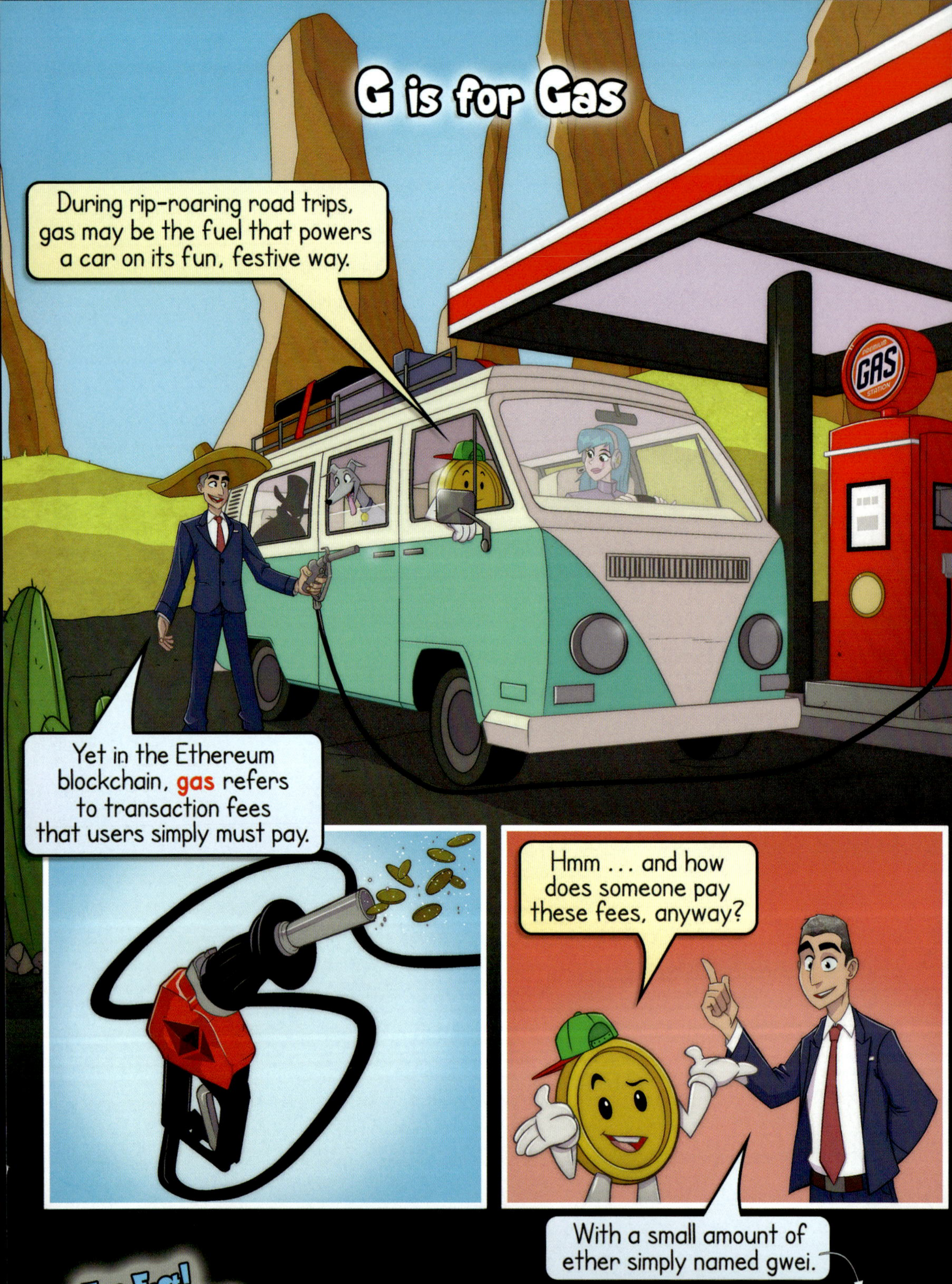

During rip-roaring road trips, gas may be the fuel that powers a car on its fun, festive way.

Yet in the Ethereum blockchain, **gas** refers to transaction fees that users simply must pay.

Hmm . . . and how does someone pay these fees, anyway?

With a small amount of ether simply named gwei.

Pronounced "gwey"

Fun Fact!
Gwei

Gwei is a very small amount of the cryptocurrency ether. Similar to a dollar having 100 pennies, 1 ether has 1,000,000,000 gwei. Gas fees are usually measured in gwei.

Scan Me for Fun Crypto Knock-Knock Joke

H is for HODL

Bitcointalk Forum
(December 18, 2013)

GameKyuubi: I am HODLING!

BitcoinBob: Dude? What did you just say?

GameKyuubi: I am HODLING!

In a Bitcoin forum not long ago, someone misspelled the word "hold."

They incorrectly typed **h-o-d-l** (that's the old rumor we're told).

The term "HODL" has stood for **"Hold On for Dear Life"** ever since that memorable day.

It's a passive crypto investment strategy— and one that's surely here to stay.

It advises you to "hold" onto your crypto assets for quite a long time,

and patiently wait and hopefully hope that their value will steadily climb.

Meet Cryptonaire Wannabe

Hey folks, I'm smooth and, good-looking and, may I say, quite debonair.

I'm HODLING my Bitcoin so I can become a rich cryptonaire.

NO, NO, NO! Being a "cryptonaire" is not just about money, I must surely declare.

Acquiring vast crypto knowledge and skills are the secrets to being a "true" cryptonaire.

Henri

Knock, knock.

Who's there?

Henri.

Henri who?

Henri Potter . . . your "Web3 Wizard."

Fun Fact! Web3

Web3 (also known as Web 3.0) refers to the 3rd generation of the World Wide Web (internet), which incorporates concepts such as blockchain technologies, decentralization, and token-based economics.

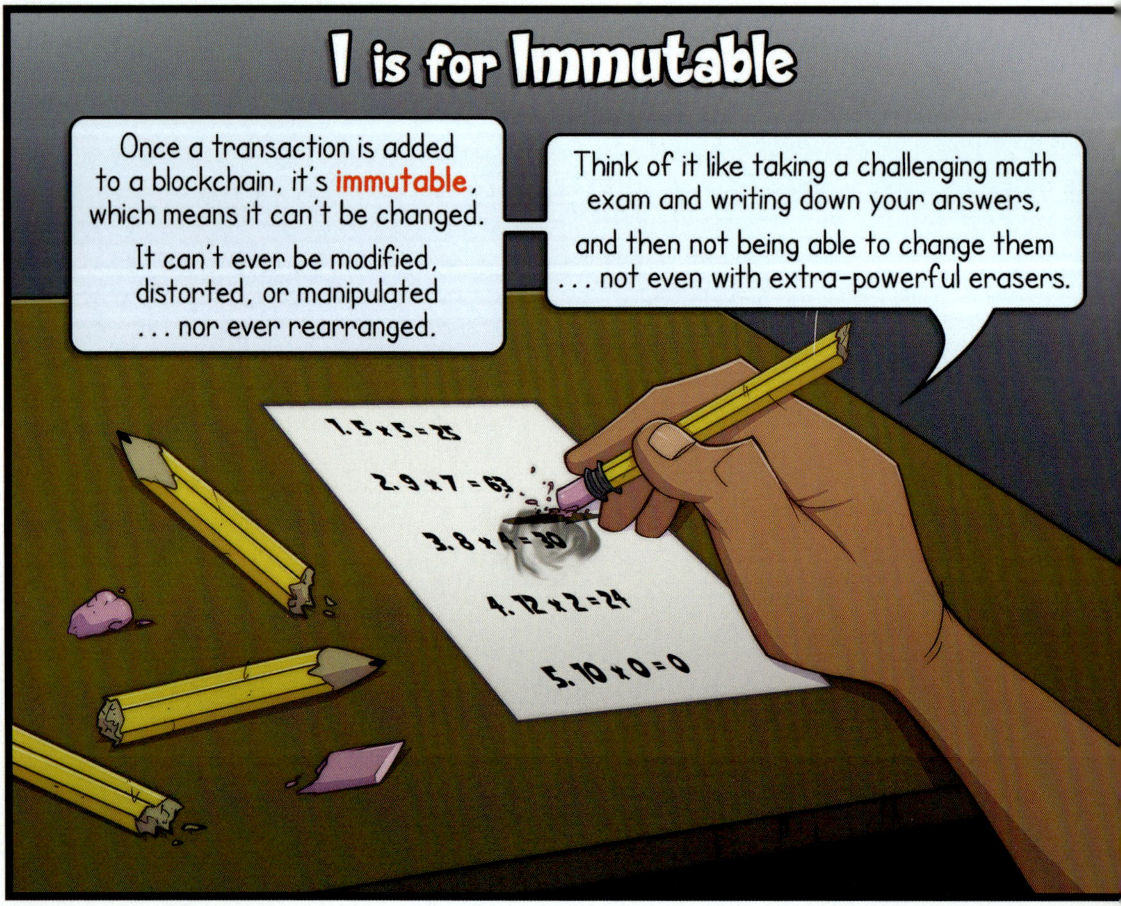

I is for Immutable

Once a transaction is added to a blockchain, it's **immutable**, which means it can't be changed.

It can't ever be modified, distorted, or manipulated . . . nor ever rearranged.

Think of it like taking a challenging math exam and writing down your answers, and then not being able to change them . . . not even with extra-powerful erasers.

1. 5 x 5 = 25
2. 9 x 7 = 63
3. 8 x 4 = 30
4. 12 x 2 = 24
5. 10 x 0 = 0

Everyone, meet Java, my jubilant pup and jolly best friend.

She's jazzy and jaunty and brings everyone great joy to no end.

And her name's the same as my favorite coding language that's just dear to my heart.

With Java, I code apps that utilize blockchain contracts—which are binding and "smart."

Fun Fact!

Java Programming Language

Scan Me for Examples of Java Code

Java is used in internet programming, app development for mobile devices, and game development. It was developed by a team of programmers led by James Gosling at Sun Microsystems in 1995. Its name is derived from Java, an island in Indonesia that is famous for its coffee. Legend has it that the name was chosen because of the programmers' love of Peet's Java coffee being consumed during their meetings.

Scan Me for a Surprise

K is for Key (Public & Private)

Typical "physical keys" allow you to access several different things,

from your home to your stinky gym locker to a secret chest safekeeping your rings.

Every crypto transaction contains two components that are critically key.

They are a "public key" and a "private key" . . . to that we cannot disagree.

One key is known only to its owner, while the other is free for anyone to see.

Okey dokey, everyone, put on your thinking caps and attempt to guess the correct key.

Which "crypto key" is known only to its owner?

Answer: ____________________

Which "crypto key" is free for everyone to see?

Answer: ____________________

Your crypto "private key" is known only to you or your allies

and keeps your crypto assets secure and away from prying eyes.

Think of a "private key" as the key that you use for your front door to unlock.

It allows you to enter, while everyone else must just respectfully knock.

Your crypto "public key"—known to all—allows anyone to send you crypto, easily and without fail.

Think of a "public key" as your home address where anyone can send you packages and all types of mail.

"Key" Challenge: How many times does the word "key" appear on this page?

Answer: ________

Henri's joke was funny ☐

Henri's joke was lame ☐

L is for Ledger (Distributed Ledger)

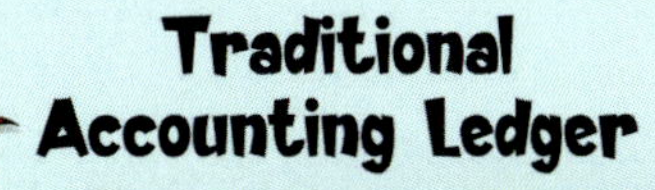

Distributed Ledger

Unlike traditional ledgers, data in distributed ledgers can't be amended.

With newer, successive transactions, distributed ledgers can only be appended.

Think of it as someone's age, and gradually growing older as time slips by.

We can't ever subtract years from our age, although some of us would sure love to try.

M is for Metaverse

A **metaverse** is a 3D digital world—a vast community with unlimited land.

An immersive, computer-generated space—truly inviting and exceptionally grand.

It's a vibrant virtual realm where one goes to explore,

creating amazing adventures like never before.

People around the world intermingle in a huge, decentralized digital place,

not constrained by their gender, background, or race . . . nor by their limiting physical space.

You enter as an "avatar" to mingle or work, to learn or to play!

With unlimited things to do and to discover each and every day.

Immersive Experiences

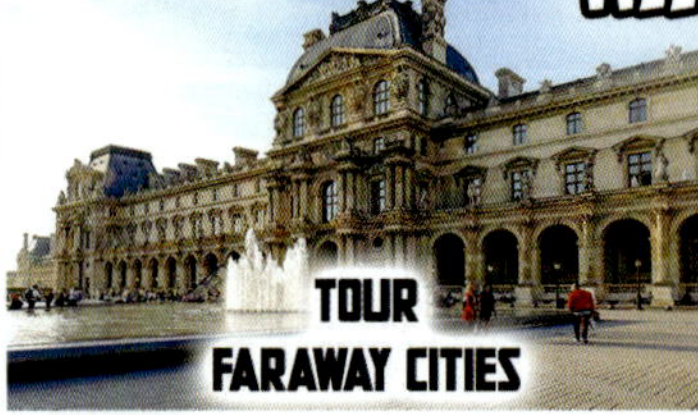

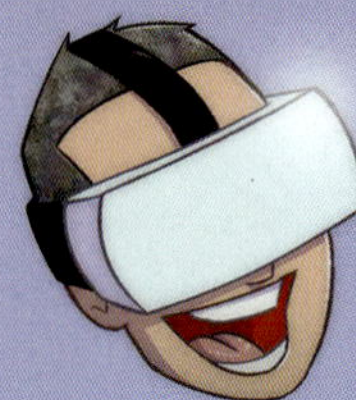

You can engage in unique experiences, do unimaginable things.

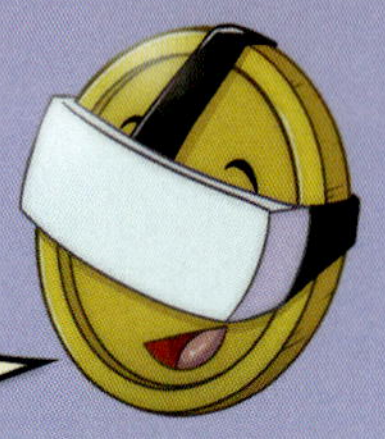

Whatsoever you can think or dream of, whatever your imagination brings.

Imagine smoothly soaring through a boundless sky amongst fearless feathered friends.
Or diving in great ocean depths where mystery begins when sunlight swiftly ends.
Or vroom-vrooming in a souped-up car 'round a super-duper speedway!
Or calmly cruising in a Lambo on an endless famous freeway.
ROUTE
66
Or ballooning with my Bitcoin buddies over fabled Phang Nga Bay.
Scan Me for More on Metaverses

N is for NFT (Non-Fungible Token)

Assets converted to electronic form

An NFT is a digital asset that's exclusive and one of a kind, from music, to video, to artwork, to cool creations distinctly designed.

Because of their unique digital signatures, no two NFTs can ever be the same. This makes each of them deservedly special, with a truly worthy claim to great worldwide fame.

NFTs also represent someone's public proof of ownership—one's indisputable receipt. A secure digitized document stored on a blockchain to prevent fraud and any dreaded deceit.

Proof of Ownership

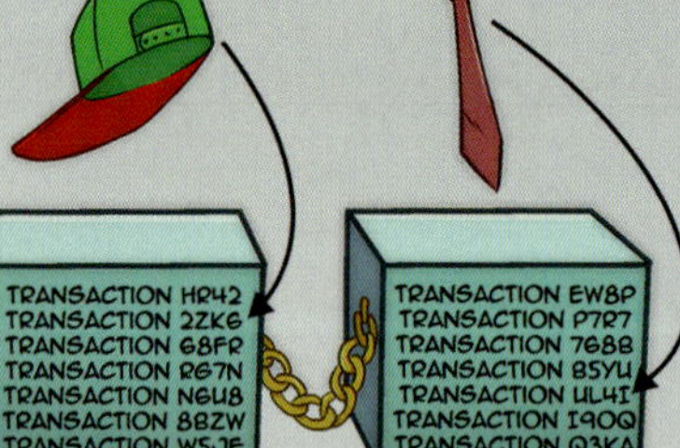

TRANSACTION ABCD
TRANSACTION DHEG
TRANSACTION 6RPV
TRANSACTION VX4X
TRANSACTION XA2Z
TRANSACTION ZKOL
TRANSACTION LYZK

TRANSACTION KQRT
TRANSACTION TY8M
TRANSACTION M9IF
TRANSACTION F7J3
TRANSACTION 3849
TRANSACTION 9U7C
TRANSACTION CHNH

TRANSACTION HR42
TRANSACTION 2ZK6
TRANSACTION 68FR
TRANSACTION R67N
TRANSACTION N6U8
TRANSACTION 88ZW
TRANSACTION WSJE

TRANSACTION EW8P
TRANSACTION P7R7
TRANSACTION 7688
TRANSACTION 85YU
TRANSACTION UL4I
TRANSACTION I9OQ
TRANSACTION Q3KA

Blockchain Transactions

Scan Me for More on NFTs

Fungible vs. Non-Fungible: Explained

For example, a Bitcoin is fungible—it's not exclusive, nor is it rare. Trade one Bitcoin for another; it's the same—no matter when and no matter where.

Non-fungible things are different—as they are rare and exclusive, and quite unique, like an autographed Satoshi card or King Arthur's striking, battle-worn antique.

Fun Fact!

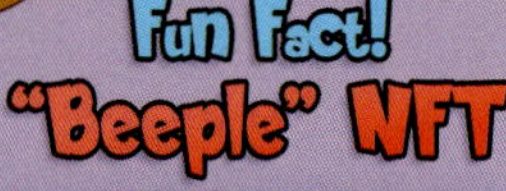

"Beeple" NFT

sold for $69.3 million at Christie's online auction on March 11, 2021.

O is for Open Source
"Open source" refers to computer code that's available to all, be it me or be it you.
It's always completely accessible to the general public, free to use and free to view.
Computer Code
FREE
It's unlike proprietary software that is owned by only one, or perhaps by just a few.
And where the code is inaccessible to the general public, be it me or be it you.
XYZ
COMPANY
Meet Open Sourcerer (Metaverse Magician)
Bitcoin's code is "open source," and thus available for everyone to use.
And, if needed, anyone is welcome to change it to anything they choose.
Think of it like a magician showing everyone how their magic tricks are done.
Revealing their clever little secrets and letting everyone in on all the fun.
Asset Exchange
P2P is an exchange of assets between two parties who agree,
without the use of middlemen, agents, or an untrustworthy trustee.
Cryptocurrency transactions are decentralized asset exchanges—P2P, of course!
The only two participants are the recipient and their very agreeable source.
P is for P2P (Peer-to-Peer)
And since crypto transactions are primarily peer-to-peer,
they may soon force some banks to shutter their doors and disappear.

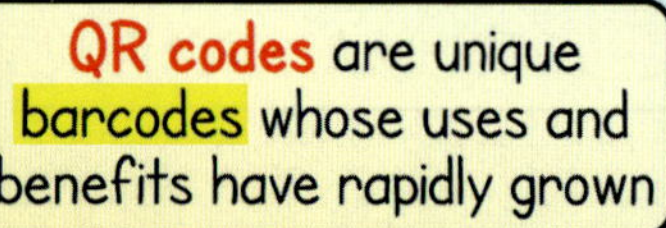

Henri & Hodler's QR Code Scavenger Hunt

Search for all the **QR Codes** scattered throughout the pages of this book and scan them with a smartphone for links to fun bonus activities . . . and to learn more cool things!

Scan Me for Naka & Moto's "Crypto Challenge"

Meet Naka (Hodler's smartphone)

Meet Moto (Henri's smartphone)

R is for Recovery Seed

When a self-custody crypto wallet is initially created, a distinctly random confidential code is promptly generated.

This code is called a "recovery seed" and contains 12, 18, or 24 simple arbitrary words.

These words can be just about anything, from speedy sports to salty snacks to a very special breed of birds.

Recovery Seed is also referred to as: seed, seed phrase, backup seed phrase, recovery phrase, mnemonic phrase, BIP-39 seed phrase.

If Henri could choose his recovery seed, below are the words he would use.

Montreal books Philippe golf
hummus work nerdy fencing
library Dubai Maria Yerevan
salsa jokester Vera capsule
Lara hockey dog chocolate
lion scuba sauna Sparky

If you could choose your recovery seed, what words would you use? Add your words below.

____ ____ ____ ____ ____ ____
____ ____ ____ ____ ____ ____
____ ____ ____ ____ ____ ____
____ ____ ____ ____ ____ ____

Scan Me for a Surprise

If you lose access to your crypto wallet, it can be very stressful, ***yes indeed!*** In order to retrieve your crypto assets, there's one essential thing that you will need.

And, the answer is . . . your one and only, and most trustworthy ol' "recovery seed." And if you know its whereabouts, retrieval of your assets is surely guaranteed.

So make sure to write it down and store it in a locked safe or in a super-secret place.

In the event you lose access to your crypto wallet, you can retrieve it, just in case.

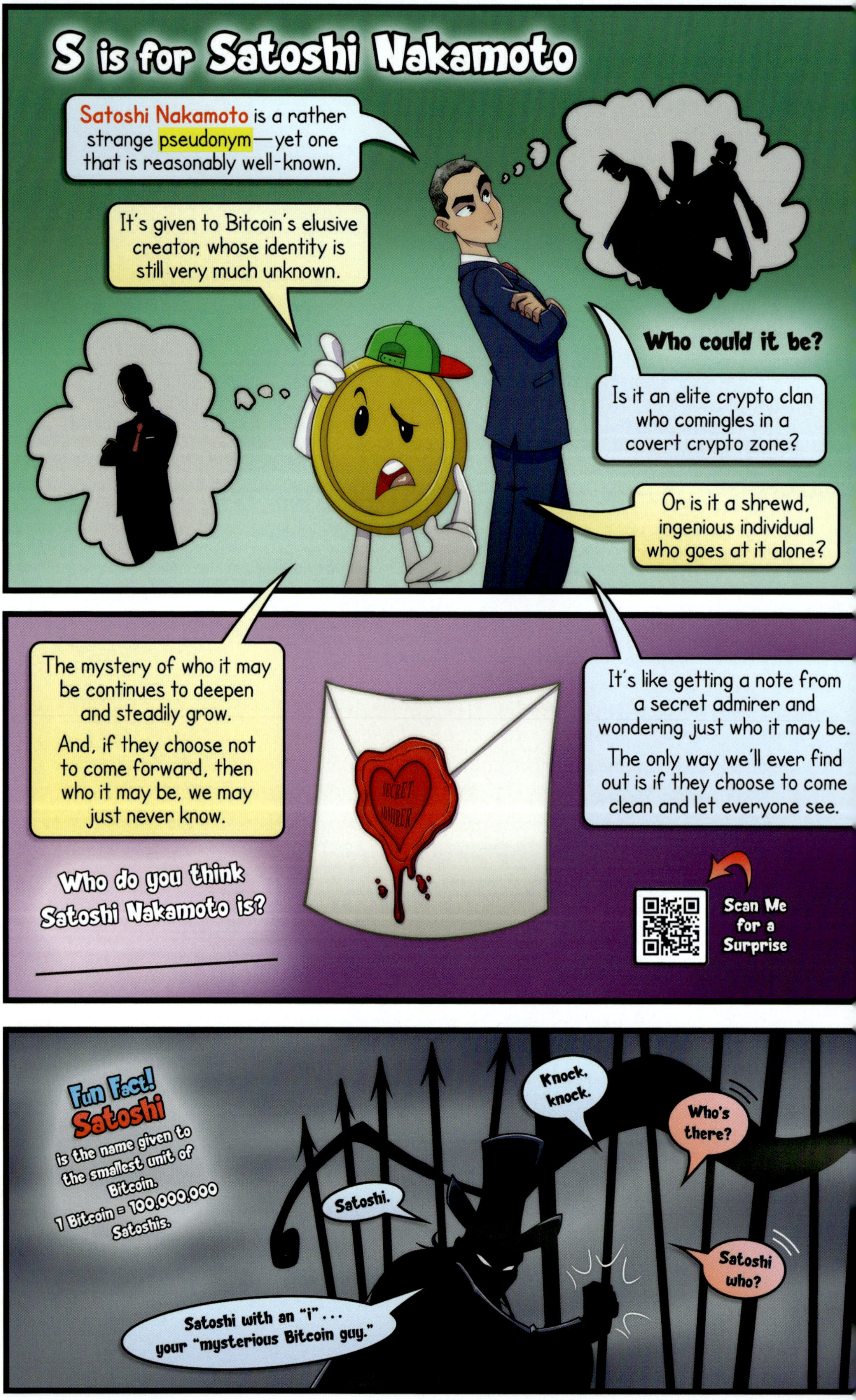

S is for Satoshi Nakamoto

Satoshi Nakamoto is a rather strange pseudonym—yet one that is reasonably well-known.

It's given to Bitcoin's elusive creator, whose identity is still very much unknown.

Who could it be?

Is it an elite crypto clan who comingles in a covert crypto zone?

Or is it a shrewd, ingenious individual who goes at it alone?

The mystery of who it may be continues to deepen and steadily grow.

And, if they choose not to come forward, then who it may be, we may just never know.

It's like getting a note from a secret admirer and wondering just who it may be.

The only way we'll ever find out is if they choose to come clean and let everyone see.

Who do you think Satoshi Nakamoto is?

____

Scan Me for a Surprise

And . . . S is for Solidity

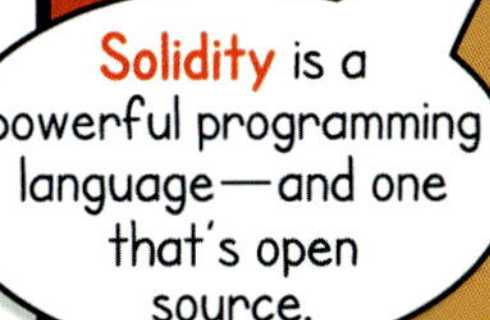

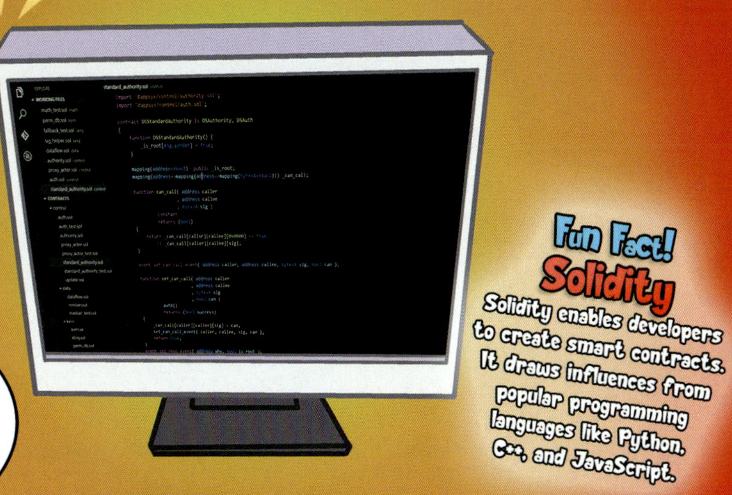

Meet Solidity

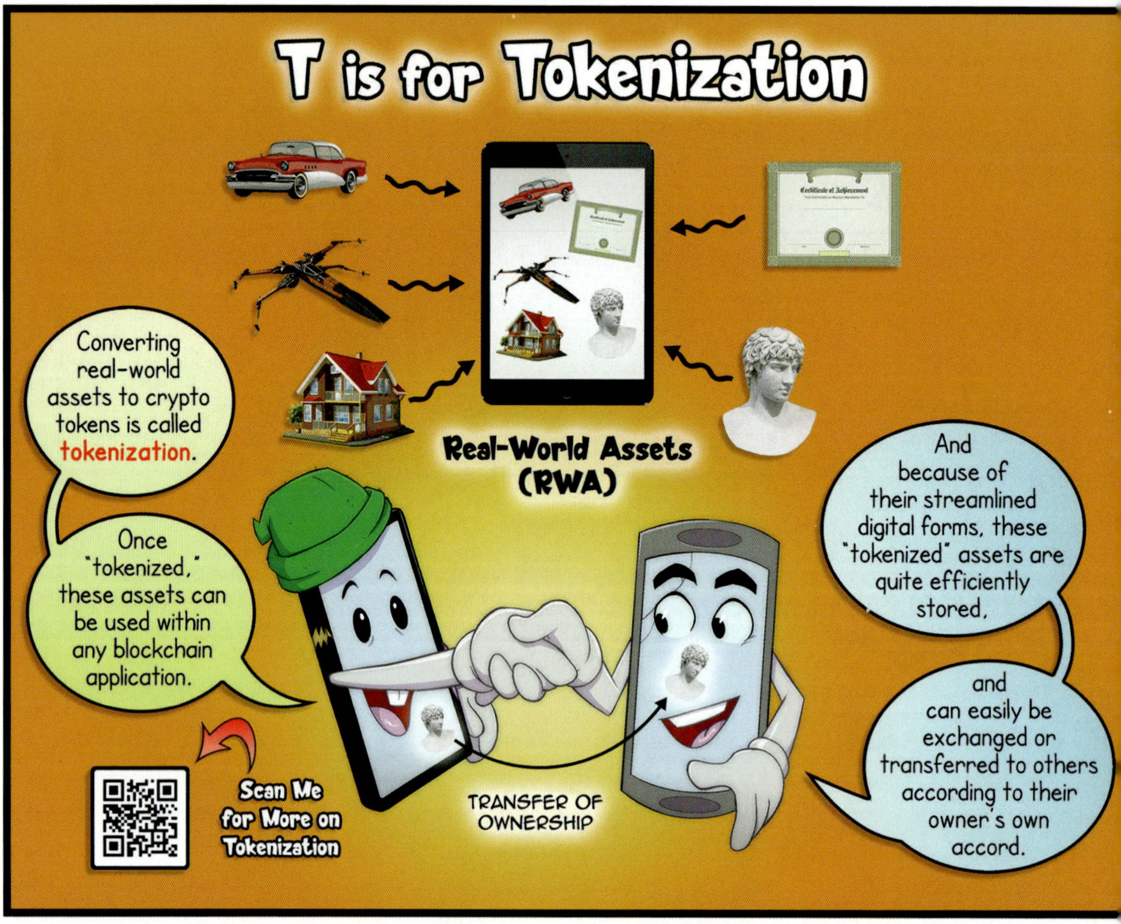

T is for Tokenization

Real-World Assets (RWA)

Converting real-world assets to crypto tokens is called **tokenization**.

Once "tokenized," these assets can be used within any blockchain application.

And because of their streamlined digital forms, these "tokenized" assets are quite efficiently stored,

and can easily be exchanged or transferred to others according to their owner's own accord.

TRANSFER OF OWNERSHIP

Scan Me for More on Tokenization

DID YOU KNOW? Tokenized assets on a blockchain come in two distinct forms: Tangible & Intangible

They're either tangible, like gold, real estate, or fine works of art.

Like a priceless oil painting of Henri's ultra-groovy go-kart.

OWNED BY HODLER

Or they're intangible, like NFTs, or someone's ownership rights.

Like a digital certificate of Hodler's huge high-flying kites.

Scan Me for a Surprise

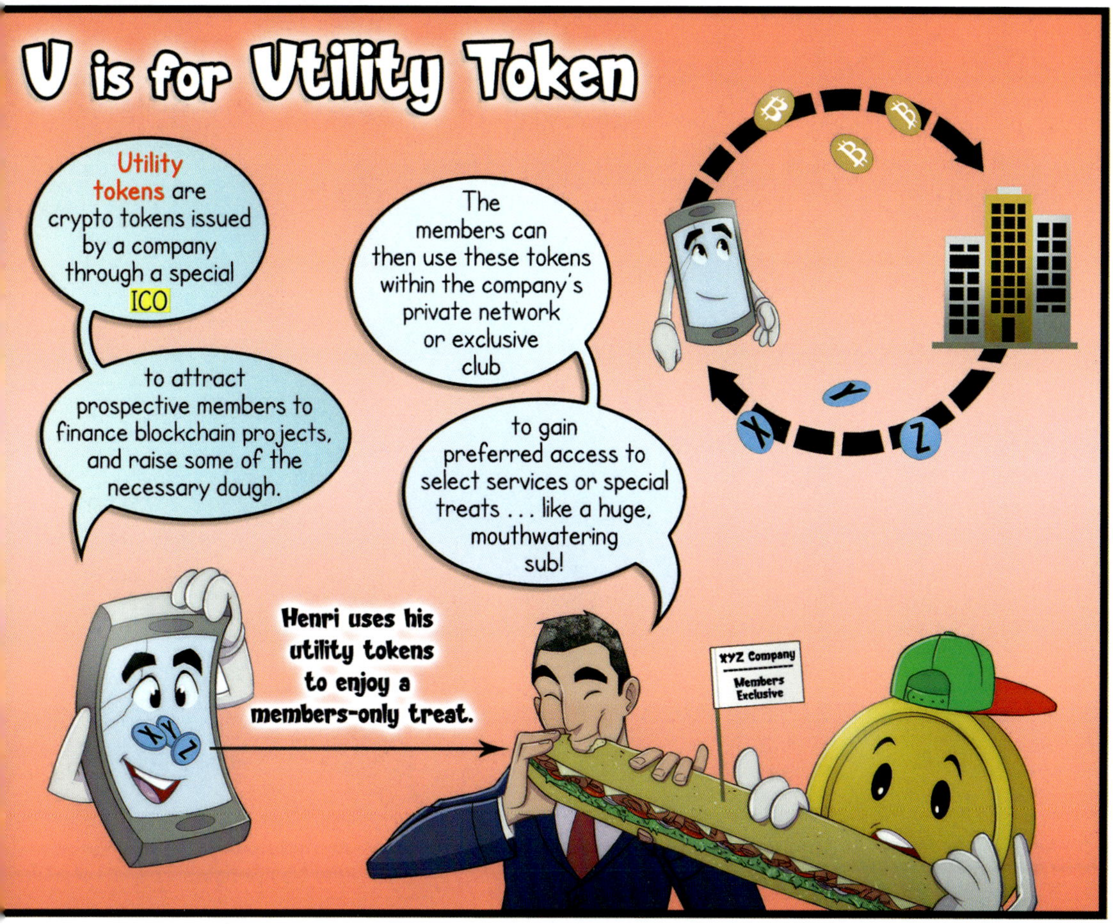

U is for Utility Token

Utility tokens are crypto tokens issued by a company through a special ICO

to attract prospective members to finance blockchain projects, and raise some of the necessary dough.

The members can then use these tokens within the company's private network or exclusive club

to gain preferred access to select services or special treats . . . like a huge, mouthwatering sub!

Henri uses his utility tokens to enjoy a members-only treat.

XYZ Company

Members Exclusive

Real-World Analogy

It's like when someone purchases advance tickets to our soon-to-open "**Web3 Wonderland**."

They'll get first access to all the rides, and unlimited cones at our "Silly Scoops" ice-cream stand.

V is for Validator

Validators perform important tasks and are crucial to a blockchain's operation.

As the "blockchain's bookkeepers," they confirm all transactions essential to its foundation.

APPROVED

APPROVED

They verify that every transaction is recorded as accurately as it should.

And they reject any shady transactions from bad people who may be up to no good.

W is for Wallet

X is for . . .
"X-tra! X-tra!"
Read all about it!

Scan Me for "Henri & Hodler in the News"

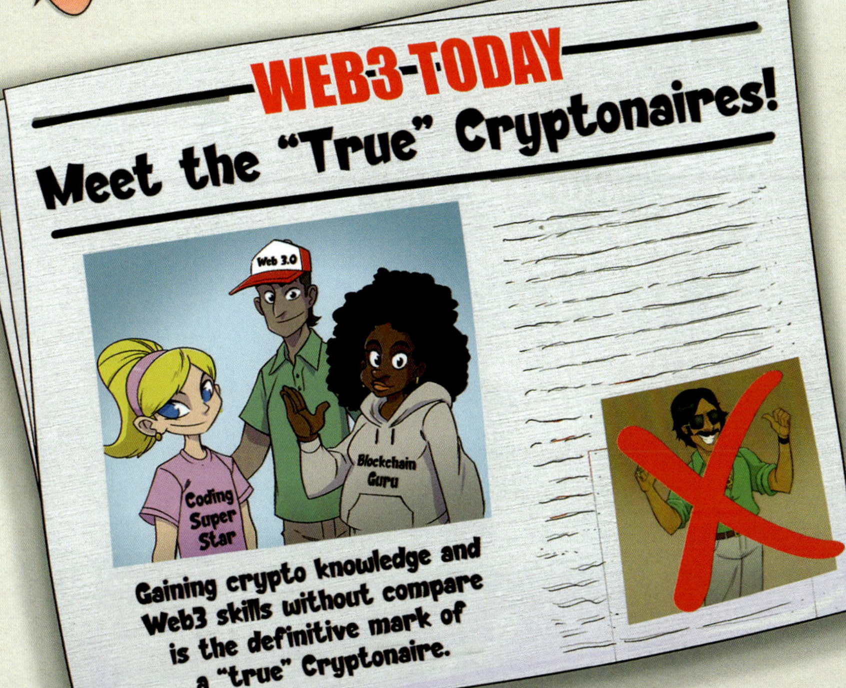

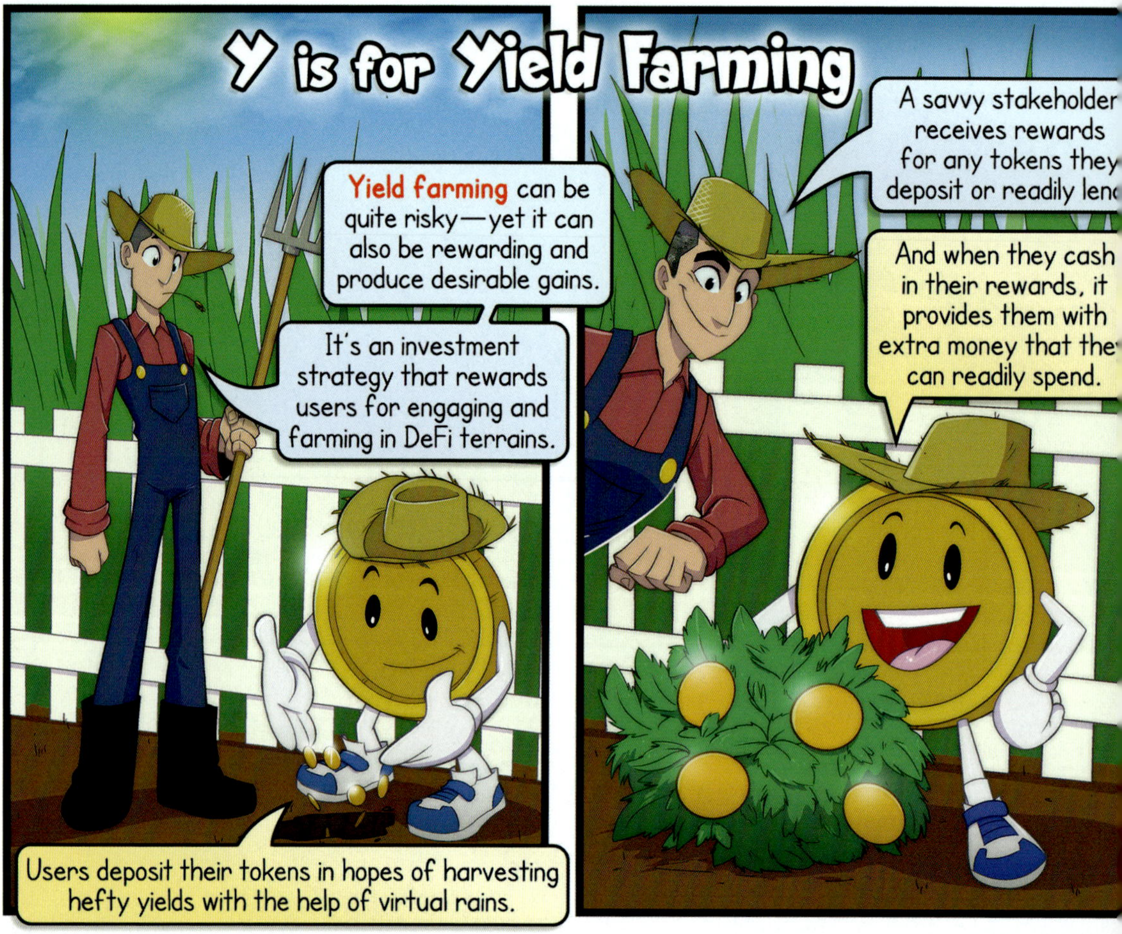

Y is for Yield Farming

Yield farming can be quite risky—yet it can also be rewarding and produce desirable gains.

It's an investment strategy that rewards users for engaging and farming in DeFi terrains.

Users deposit their tokens in hopes of harvesting hefty yields with the help of virtual rains.

A savvy stakeholder receives rewards for any tokens they deposit or readily len

And when they cash in their rewards, it provides them with extra money that the can readily spend.

Z is for ZK Proof (Zero Knowledge)

ZK Proof is used in many blockchain platforms and is a crafty form of cryptographic proof.

It ensures data privacy, just how a house provides privacy through soundproof walls and a sturdy roof.

It verifies "truth of information" without revealing the actual information itself.

Just how by observing Henri's belly, I can tel if he's hungry or simply overstuffed himself.

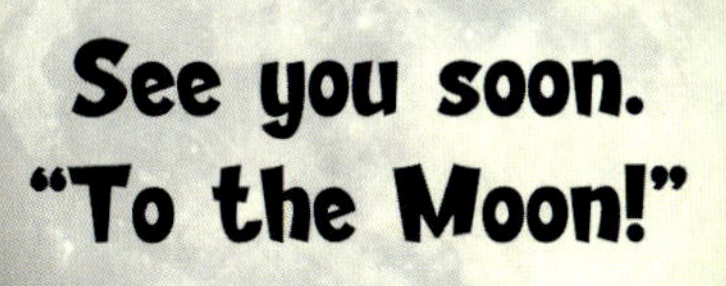
See you soon.
"To the Moon!"

Fun Fact!
"To the Moon"
is a reference to a cryptocurrency's potential to substantially increase in value over time and result in a huge profit.

Well folks, there you have it, **Decoding Crypto** all the way from **"A to Z."**
We taught terms from "altcoin" to "ZK Proof" enjoyably and easily.
ADD YOUR PICTURE HERE
Future of Money Club
Congrats! You're now an official member of our club and cool crypto crew.
And we've prepared more great lessons, so come back real soon to learn something new.

G is for Glossary

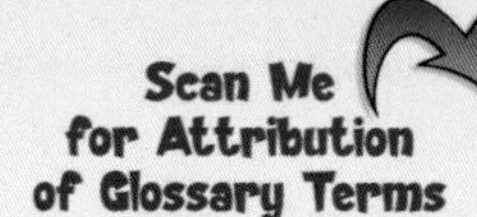

A

Asset – a single item of ownership having exchange value; something of value

Autonomous(ly) – existing or capable of existing independently

B

Barcode – a code consisting of a group of variously sized, patterned bars, lines, and spaces that contains information about the object or product it labels and is scanned and read by an optical scanner or mobile app

Barter – the act of trading goods or services for other goods or services

Bitcoin Forum – a gathering of individuals (usually online) who meet to express their views, opinions, and concerns about Bitcoin and the Bitcoin ecosystem

C

Coding Language – a system of notation or language used to write computer programs, which are sets of instructions for digital devices (e.g., computers, smartphones, tablets) to execute

Commerce – the exchange or buying and selling of commodities on a large scale involving transportation from place to place

Computer Code – a set of instructions written in a programming language for a digital device to execute (as within a piece of software)

Cryptocurrency – any form of digital currency that relies on cryptography for security, uses a decentralized system to record transactions, and that usually has no central issuing or regulating authority

Cryptographic Proof – a mathematical proof using a cryptographic hash function that verifies that a message has not been tampered with and that can be verified by someone who has access to the original message and the proof

Cryptosphere – the blockchain-based univers which includes digital currencies, smart contracts, crypto exchanges, and all their supporting services

Cryptoverse – same definition as Cryptospher (see above)

Currency – something that is in circulation and is used as a medium of exchange; money

D

Decentralized – the dispersion of functions and powers; run by a distributed network of users and not by any single authority like a government or bank

Digital Age – the present time, in which man things are done by computer and large amounts of information are available because of computer technology

Digital Asset – anything of value that is stored and transmitted electronically throug a digital device and is associated with ownership or use rights

Digital Signature – a secure method of linkin an identity to digital data through the use o cryptography and encryption

Distributed Network – a network of users tha spreads work across multiple sources and efficiently shares resources

E

Economy – activities related to the consumption, production, and trade of goods and services as an ongoing functioning systen

Encryption – the act or process of converting sensitive information or data to prevent unauthorized access

Exchange – the act of giving or taking one thing in return for another

F

inance – the system that includes the irculation of money, the granting of credit, he making of investments, and the provision f banking facilities

inancial – of or relating to matters dealing ith money and credit

inancial Ledger – a reporting system that a usiness uses to keep track of its financial ransactions and to prepare financial reports

orge – to form something (such as metal) by eating and hammering

I

CO (Initial Coin Offering) – an initial offering f a cryptocurrency to the public

ntangible (Asset) – assets that don't hysically exist, yet have a monetary value ecause they represent potential revenue .g., copyright to a song)

ntermediary – a midway agent or agency; go-between or mediator

M

ledium of Exchange – something commonly ccepted in exchange for goods and services nd recognized as representing a standard f value

liddleman – an intermediary or agent etween two parties

lint – to make (coins, money, etc.) by tamping metal

P

rogrammable – something (e.g., a computer r system) that accepts instructions via a oding language to perform a range of tasks

roprietary Software – software that is opyrighted and bears limits against use, istribution, and modification that are nposed by its publisher or developer

seudonym – a fictitious name used by omeone to conceal their identity

S

Self-Custody Crypto Wallet – a digital wallet where you keep total control of your cryptocurrencies and other digital assets, such as Bitcoin, Ethereum, etc.

Sequentially – one after the other; chronologically, or according to numerical, alphabetical, or some other recognized order

Stakeholder – anyone that has an interest or participates in a blockchain and can either affect or be affected by the blockchain's operations and management

T

Tangible (Asset) – any physical item owned by an entity (e.g., a person or company) that has a monetary value

Trade – the act of buying, selling, or exchanging commodities or property

U

Utility – having (or made for) several useful or practical purposes rather than a single, specialized one

V

Virtual – being on or simulated on a digital device (e.g., a computer); occurring or existing primarily online

W

Wallet Address – a randomly generated unique string of characters that acts as an identifier for a digital wallet

White Paper – an informational document that promotes or highlights the features of a solution, product, or service

A is for Appendix 1:
Fun Facts on Money & Finance

Early Forms of Money

Objects that are scarce in nature and whose circulation could be efficiently controlled emerged as units of value for interactions and exchange. These included mother-of-pea shells circulating in the Americas and cowrie shells that were used in Africa, Europe, Asi and Australia. Native copper, meteorites, obsidian, copper, gold, silver, and lead ingots ar several metals that have served as currency throughout history. Until recently, people have even used live animals, such as cows, as a form of currency. Whale teeth, salt, amber, beads, and cocoa beans were various other forms of money used in different parts of the world.

Cowrie Shells

Cowrie shells were one of the longest and most widely used currencies in history. They are the shells of sea snails produced by certain species of marine gastropod mollusks. These small, glossy shells are found in warm tropical oceans worldwide and were prized for their beauty, durability, and rarity in certain regions.

Origin of the Word "Money"

The word "money" originates from the Latin word "moneta," which originally referred to the temple of Juno Moneta in ancient Rome. This temple was used as a mint where Roman coins were produced. Over time, the term "moneta" came to be associated with coinage and eventually evolved into the word "money" in English and other languages.

Origin of the Word "Salary"

The word "salary" comes from the ancient Romans when they used salt as a medium of exchange. Roman soldiers were sometimes paid in salt, which is where the word "salary" originates (from the Latin word "salarium," meaning "pertaining to salt"). Why salt? Refrigeration didn't exist then, and Romans used salt to preserve food, which made salt extremely valuable.

Gold

Gold has been discovered on every continent on Earth except Antarctica.

History of Credit Cards

Credit cards were developed in the U.S. in the 1920s and were issued by individual businesses, such as oil companies and hotel chains, to their customers, and only for purchases made at company outlets. The first consumer credit card came in 1950 when Diners Club founders Ralph Schneider and Frank McNamara issued a credit card that could be used at various establishments for purchase of a variety of goods and services. The Diners Club card started the modern credit card era. Soon after, in 1958, American Express debuted their first consumer credit card.

Oldest Currency Still in Use

The oldest currency still in use is the British pound. It dates to 775 CE and was called the "pound sterling," as Anglo-Saxon kings used silver pennies, or sterlings, as money.

rigin of the Word "Bank"

he word "bank" originates from the Old Italian word "banca," which referred to a ench or table. In medieval Italy, money lenders and money changers conducted their usiness in marketplaces seated at benches or tables. Over time, the term "banca" came be associated with these financial activities.

arliest Banks

he earliest banks were ancient religious temples because they were seen as safe places to tore money. In these temples, people stored grain or other precious metals that were lso used as money.

oins with Human Images on Them

he Romans were the first to stamp the image of a living person on a coin. After inning in war, Julius Caesar featured his portrait on a coin in 44 BCE.

irst Official Currency

he first coins with their value printed on them were minted around 600 BCE in ancient ydia (now modern-day Turkey) and are believed to be the first official currency.

ighest Money Denomination Printed

he government of Hungary printed the highest denomination ever created in 1946 uring the worst case of hyperinflation ever recorded in the country. It was a bank ote worth 100 quintillion pengos: 100,000,000,000,000,000,000.

Jhat is U.S. Paper Money Made From?

.S. paper money is not paper. It's cloth, made from a blend of mostly cotton and nen. During the 1700s, people repaired torn bills with a needle and thread.

rinting of Money in the United States

n the United States, before the Federal Reserve was reated in 1913, each bank printed its own money.

ifespan of Bills

he typical lifespan of a $1 bill is less than 2 years, et $100 bills live between 9 to 15 years. All bills are ecycled when they are worn out.

lobal Currency (Physical vs. Digital)

nly 8% of global currency is actual physical money. ver 90% of the world's currency is digital in the orm of credit cards, debit cards, online purchases, nd cryptocurrency.

A is for Appendix 2:
Fun Facts on Crypto

Bitcoin Mining
The last Bitcoin will be mined in the year 2140. Only 21 million Bitcoin can ever be produced, as that number is built into Bitcoin's code. As of 2024, 19 million have been mined, and because of the way Bitcoin mining works, the number of Bitcoins that can be mined gets halved every four years. This means that although almost 90% of the total possible Bitcoin is already in circulation, it will take another 120 years or so to produce the remaining 2.2 million coins.

Crypto Ownership
As of 2023, the UAE (United Arab Emirates) leads in terms of cryptocurrency ownership as a percentage of its population, with 27.67% of its residents holding crypto.

Bitcoin as Legal Tender
On Sept. 7, 2021, El Salvador became the first country to accept Bitcoin as legal tender. Bitcoin joined the U.S. dollar as a form of payment in the country.

Missing Bitcoin
According to crypto data firm Chainalysis, around 20% of Bitcoin has been lost or is stuck in wallets that can't be accessed. Today, that equates to 3.76 million BTC. About 1.1 million BTC is held by Bitcoin's anonymous creator, Satoshi Nakamoto, and many believe that Nakamoto won't ever touch those coins. In addition, some people passed away without sharing access to their Bitcoin, which accounts for another chunk of out-of-circulation coins. Lastly, lost crypto keys are also to blame for missing Bitcoin. Crypto keys are like a bank account PIN, and you need them to access or trade your coins. Unfortunately, if you lose your keys, you're unlikely to see those coins again.

Hardware Crypto Wallets
One of the safest ways to store your crypto assets offline are hardware crypto wallets, as they're difficult to hack. But if you lose the wallet, the password, or the recovery seed, it's bye-bye crypto. There are several unfortunate stories of people losing their wallets. One person in the U.K. believes his hard drive containing 7,500 BTC is at his local garbage dump site and has been trying to get permission to search there for years.

Secret Messages on the Bitcoin Blockchain
During its IPO (initial public offering) on April 14, 2021, Coinbase—a publicly traded, global company that operates a cryptocurrency exchange platform—published a secret message on the Bitcoin blockchain as an homage to Satoshi Nakamoto, who also embedded a secret message in the very first Bitcoin block that was mined on January 3, 2009. Both hidden messages make references to massive levels of government spending, which many in the crypto community believe will lead to the continued devaluation of fiat paper money and an increase in the price of Bitcoin. Although Satoshi started the trend, other crypto miners have also used hidden messages for marking notable events in Bitcoin history. Some miners have even embedded secret messages from marriage proposals to tributes to their heroes and world-changers.

COMING SOON
Stay tuned
for more books in
the Henri & Hodler
crypto-education
book series.

About the Creators

Henri Arslanian

email: henri@henriarslanian.com

A lawyer and banker by background, Henri Arslanian has been active in the crypto space since 2014 in various leadership roles, from launching a crypto hedge fund and leading PwC's global crypto team to teaching the world's first crypto university course and sharing insights with his 500,000+ LinkedIn followers. He is the author of numerous bestselling books on crypto and fintech, including *The Book of Crypto*, and *The Future of Finance*. He decided to write this book after his daughter thought he worked for a company called Bitcoin.

Michael Dotsikas

email: michael@michaeldotsikas.com

Michael Dotsikas is the author of the award-winning and critically acclaimed Benjamin Birdie Children's Picture Book Series. His ambition in co-authoring the Henri & Hodler book series is to teach children and adults the often difficult concepts of crypto,

"in a fun, friendly, and responsible way, since it's changing the world and is here to stay!"

Although not as mysterious as Satoshi Nakamoto, Michael occasionally enjoys watching real-life mystery shows—when he's not writing witty rhymes

Billy Martin

email: info@thebillymartin.com

Billy Martin is best known as the lead guitarist for the multi-platinum selling band Good Charlotte. Aside from music, he works as a character designer and illustrator. Billy has worked for several companies, including Disney, Marvel, Nickelodeon, Hasbro, and more.

Education Partner:

First Digital